PINK DRINKS

PINK DRINKS

A COLLECTION OF FUN, FLIRTY & FRIVOLOUS COCKTAILS

KATHERINE BEBO

LONDON • NEW YORK

For Chaz, Les and Fran, with whom
I've shared many a pink drink over
the years. Love you gals!

Design Geoff Borin
Commissioning Editor Stephanie Milner
Production Meskerem Berhane
Art Director Leslie Harrington
Editorial Director Julia Charles

Styling and photographic art direction
Luis Peral
Drinks stylist Daniel Warner
Indexer Hilary Bird

First published in 2014
by Ryland Peters & Small
20–21 Jockey's Fields
London WC1R 4BW
and
519 Broadway, 5th Floor
New York, NY 10012

www.rylandpeters.com

10 9 8 7 6 5 4 3 2 1

Text © Hannah Miles, Louise Pickford, Ben
Reed, and Ryland Peters & Small 2014
Design and photography
copyright © Ryland Peters & Small

ISBN: 978-1-84975-500-9

A CIP record for this book is available
from the British Library.

Library of Congress Cataloging-in-
Publication data has been applied for.

Printed in China

RECIPE CREDITS

Hannah Miles
Berry Smoothie
Chocolate Cherry Freeze
Raspberry Ripple Float
Rose Petal Dream
 Milkshake
Watermelon Cooler

Louise Pickford
Berry Cordial
Classic Sangria
Cosmopolitan Iced Tea
Cranberry Fruit Punch
Cranberry, Lemon &
 Ginger Iced Tea
Grapefruit Rose Sparkle
Hamptons Hangover
Mango and Berry Pash
Peach & Strawberry Sangria
Raspberry & Apple Fizz
Raspberry, Apple &
 Lychee Juice
Sea Breeze
Strawberry Mule
Strawberry, Rose & Vanilla
 Iced Tea

Ben Reed
Absolutely Fabulous
Bacardi Cocktail
Bay Breeze
Berry Caipiroska
Blood Martini
Classic Cosmopolitan
Clover Club
Commodore Cocktail
Cosmo Royale
Dark and Strawmy
Diablo
Fresh Watermelon &
 Cinnamon Punch
Gin Bramble
Legend
Hibiscus Martini
Kir Royale
The Knickerbocker
Metropolitan
Pomegranate Martini
Pomegranate Punch
Pontberry Martini
Raspberry Martini
Raspberry Rickey
Red Cactus
Rude Cosmopolitan
Silk Stocking

Sloe Gin Fizz
Strawberry Martini
Rossini
Tom Collins
Triple Goddess
Watermelon Martini

PICTURE CREDITS

All photography by
Gareth Morgans with
the following exceptions:

Kate Whitaker
Pages 2, 120, 123, 124
and 127

William Lingwood
Pages 30, 37, 42, 73, 75,
88, 92, 95, 96, 103, 107,
108, 111 and 116

All illustrations by **Rob
Merrett** with the following
exceptions:

Selina Snow
Pages 16 and 17

CONTENTS

THE MAGIC OF MINXOLOGY

Pink is the colour of fun. And what's more fun than getting together with your gals and drinking in all the merriment you can? If you're looking to host a girly party – sparkles and all – this book will quench all of your 'What drinks shall I serve?' frets. From a hen do/bachelorette party to a baby shower, a girls' brunch to a summer tea party, we've got every pink occasion covered with suggestions of what drinks to offer – be they cocktails, mocktails, iced tea, shakes, punch, smoothies or coolers.

The joys of sociable drinking can't be underestimated. Sitting with your besties, cocktail in hand, nattering about new jobs, nights out, naughty boys and general nonsense can't fail to make you smile. And if the cocktail so happens to be pink, make that smile a grin, beam or all-out whoop. Yes, the power of pink knows no bounds.

Throughout this book, you'll discover how to become a 'minxologist' overnight, with tips on how to stock your bar and how to serve your enchanting creations. Also pick up suggestions on how to decorate for your pink party, plus what food to serve. If you want your party to sparkle, shimmer, glimmer and glow, Pink Drinks is bubbling with ideas. Now, without further ado, let's clink to the pink!

PERFECTLY PINK HOSTESS

★

Before we get to the main attraction – the drinks – let's ponder the rest of the party for a moment. To complement the scrumptious liquid creations, you could offer pink nibbles. Indulge a sweet tooth with cupcakes, candy floss/cotton candy, marshmallows, meringues, lollipops and bubble gum. Or serve more 'substantial' bites such as prawns, smoked salmon and radish salad. To display the food, you could buy ceramic 'letter' dishes that spell 'P-I-N-K'.

Decorate with pink flower arrangements – roses, tulips, orchids, peonies, carnations, gerberas, hydrangeas, lilies, sweet peas, pansies... anything goes, just as long as the petals pack a pretty punch. Adding glitter to the flower water will add a twinkly twist. You could also display pink balloons, scatter pink confetti, light pink candles, use pink tableware, suspend pink paper lanterns, string up pink fairy lights... or decorate with anything else that'd make Princess Barbie proud. No frills? No way! The frillier and more feminine, the better. The beauty of pink is that there are so many shades – from pastel to hot, shocking to cerise, and every tint in-between. You could call it your '50 Shades of Pink' party.

If you're looking for musical inspiration, create a playlist with tunes such as Pink Cadillac by Bruce Springsteen, Pink by Aerosmith or anything by Pink and Pink Floyd. Heck, you could even play the Pink Panther theme tune! Whatever direction your fabulous party takes – go delicate, go loud or go girl! – one thing's for sure: serve your guests any one of the fun, flirty, frivolous drinks from this book and they'll be tickled pink.

HOW PINK IS YOUR DRINK?

Just how pink do you want your party to be? Do you want it to be a pretty, pastel affair or an in-your-face, fuchsia fandango? What's the most important factor to you when it comes to serving bevvies of the blush variety? The fun factor? Feisty factor? Fabulous factor? Fresh factor? Or a fizzy mixture of all four? Use this chart to plan your bash and then prepare to take your guests to the brink with pink!

Fun = A taste or decoration with a little *je ne sais quoi*
Feisty = Booze content
Fabulous = Wouldn't be out of place on the set of *Sex And The City*
Fresh = Fruity-licious

Drink	Fun	Feisty	Fabulous	Fresh	Pink Power
SHIRLEY TEMPLE (PAGE 44)	2	0	2	2	6
CRANBERRY, LEMON & GINGER ICED TEA (PAGE 106)	3	0	2	1	6
SLOE GIN FIZZ (PAGE 72)	2	2	2	1	7
DARK & STRAWMY (PAGE 40)	2	2	2	1	7
SEA BREEZE (PAGE 23)	2	2	2	2	8
BACARDI COCKTAIL (PAGE 39)	2	3	2	1	8
LEGEND (PAGE 24)	3	2	2	1	8
CLOVER CLUB (PAGE 27)	3	2	2	1	8
METROPOLITAN (PAGE 48)	2	2	3	1	8
BERRY CAIPIROSKA (PAGE 36)	2	1	2	3	8
HAMPTONS HANGOVER (PAGE 79)	3	1	3	1	8
GRAPEFRUIT ROSE SPARKLE (PAGE 80)	4	0	2	2	8
CLASSIC SANGRIA (PAGE 86)	2	3	2	1	8
TRIPLE GODDESS (PAGE 90)	4	0	2	2	8
CRANBERRY & FRUIT PUNCH (PAGE 98)	2	0	2	4	8
BERRY CORDIAL (PAGE 110)	2	0	2	4	8
CHOCOLATE CHERRY FREEZE (PAGE 122)	5	0	2	1	8

Drink	Fun	Feisty	Fabulous	Fresh	Pink Power
GIN BRAMBLE (PAGE 28)	3	2	2	2	9
COMMODORE COCKTAIL (PAGE 43)	3	2	3	1	9
MANGO BERRY PASH (PAGE 118)	3	0	1	5	9
RASPBERRY & APPLE FIZZ (PAGE 83)	3	0	2	4	9
BAY BREEZE (PAGE 101)	2	2	3	2	9
RASPBERRY RIPPLE (PAGE 125)	5	0	2	2	9
ROSE PETAL DREAM MILKSHAKE (PAGE 121)	5	0	3	1	9
ROSSINI (PAGE 64)	2	1	4	2	9
STRAWBERRY, ROSE & VANILLA ICED TEA (PAGE 109)	5	0	2	2	9
RASPBERRY, APPLE & LYCHEE JUICE (PAGE 114)	3	0	1	5	9
WATERMELON COOLER (PAGE 126)	3	0	1	5	9
THE KNICKERBOCKER (PAGE 31)	3	2	2	3	10
DIABLO (PAGE 32)	4	3	2	1	10
RASPBERRY RICKY (PAGE 71)	3	3	3	1	10
TOM COLLINS (PAGE 93)	3	3	2	2	10
CLASSIC COSMOPOLITAN (PAGE 20)	2	2	5	1	10
PONTBERRY MARTINI (PAGE 51)	2	2	4	2	10
WATERMELON MARTINI (PAGE 55)	2	2	4	2	10
CHEESECAKE MARTINI (PAGE 60)	2	2	4	2	10
COSMOPOLITAN ICED TEA (PAGE 105)	3	3	3	1	10
RED CACTUS (PAGE 35)	3	4	2	2	11
WATERMELON & CINNAMON PUNCH (PAGE 94)	5	0	2	4	11
POMEGRANATE PUNCH (PAGE 97)	3	2	3	3	11
STRAWBERRY MULE (PAGE 76)	4	3	2	2	11
BERRY SMOOTHIE (PAGE 117)	5	0	1	5	11
RASPBERRY MARTINI (PAGE 52)	3	2	4	3	12
COSMO ROYALE (PAGE 67)	3	2	5	2	12
ABSOLUTELY FABULOUS (PAGE 68)	3	2	5	2	12
KIR ROYALE (PAGE 75)	2	5	4	1	12
PEACH & STRAWBERRY SANGRIA (PAGE 89)	4	3	2	3	12
SILK STOCKING (PAGE 102)	4	3	4	1	12
BLOOD MARTINI (PAGE 59)	4	4	4	2	14
HIBISCUS MARTINI (PAGE 56)	5	3	4	2	14

MINXING
ESSENTIALS

Think mixing a cocktail looks like too much hard work? All that pre-chilling, muddling, crushing, stirring, straining, pouring... phew! You don't have to go all Coyote Ugly in order to make the perfect drink. All you need is a little spirit (both figuratively and, of course, literally).

The basic spirits you should keep stocked in your at-home bar are: vodka, gin, rum, tequila and whisky. You'll also want some orange liqueur (triple sec, Cointreau, Grand Marnier), berry liqueur (crème de framboise, crème de cassis, crème de mure, Chambord), peach schnapps and Campari, as well as some champagne to give certain drinks a little fizz. Many cocktails also call for either sugar syrup or sugar. Keep fruit juices such as orange, cranberry, grapefruit, apple, pomegranate, lemon and lime on hand – plus soda water, tonic water, ginger beer and lemonade.

A cocktail's not a cocktail without a garnish, so have some lemons, limes, oranges, raspberries, cherries, strawberries and redcurrants to hand to create a wonderful finishing touch. A straw and mini umbrella wouldn't go amiss either. For the Sassy Shakes & Smoothies chapter, stock up on delectable dairy with milk, cream, yogurt and ice cream.

Then it's just a matter of following the recipes and trying not to swig from the bottles as you go. See? Simple. There's really no need to feel intimidated as you take the brave, exciting steps towards becoming a minxologist. When it comes to whipping up tasty treats from your bar, remember that you're the one calling the shots.

MINXING TOOLS

It's not like you need 19 different eye shadows, 102 pairs of shoes and 43 handbags... but they're fun to have, right? To the same end, while you don't strictly need lots of bartending equipment to mix a delicious pink drink, how much cooler would it be to stock your home bar with all the right gear? Pick and choose what you'd like to have from these bar accessories... then go play.

Measure/Jigger

Measures/jiggers come in a variety of sizes so you can pour the correct quantity of drink. The dual measure is a good choice, where one end holds 25 ml and the other holds 50 ml in the UK, or ½ oz and 1 oz in the US.

Shaker

Shake it up, baby, now! There are two basic types of shaker – the three-piece (or deco) shaker and the Boston shaker. They come in all shapes and sizes, from fire extinguishers to rockets, penguins to penises!

Mixing Glass

This is used for making drinks that are stirred, not shaken.

Bar Spoon

Handy for both stirring drinks and for the gentle
pouring required for layering drinks. The flat end
can be used for muddling or crushing ingredients too.

Muddler

A long pestle that's used for mixing or
crushing ingredients such as sugar cubes,
lemons or limes.

Strainer

There are two types of strainer – the Hawthorn strainer
that will sit over the metal part of the shaker, and
the Julep that fits comfortably in the mixing glass.

Straws

A simple straw is a hygienic way to test the taste of your tipple. Dip it
into the drink and place your finger over the top end to create a
vacuum. Take the straw out and suck the liquid to see if it needs
anything to be added.

Blender

To whizz up your drinks to within an inch of their lives.

Juicer

Useful when extracting the juice from citrus fruits.

Swizzle Sticks

Used for stirring drinks. Plus it's fun to say.

MINXING
GLASSWARE

With everything in life, it's all in the presentation (you wouldn't leave the house without a slick of lip gloss, would you?), and the same applies with serving drinks. Why use some sad, plastic beaker when you can use a pretty glass that will display your beautiful creation in its best light? The following glasses should be all you need to show off your taste sensations with gorgeous gusto.

If you want to gussy the glasses up, you could use stick-on jewels, temporary tattoos, glittery transfers, glass charms or thin wire to attach sequins, tiny gems or small buttons around the rim or stem. Girl, now it's time to kick some glass!

Shot Glass
Pretty self-explanatory, this small glass holds either a single or a double shot.

Tumbler
Also known as an old-fashioned glass, rocks glass or lowball glass, a tumbler is used for drinks served on the rocks (short drinks over ice).

Highball Glass
This is a tall, thin glass used for serving long cocktails.

Martini Glass

Dita Von Teese and Betty Boop would be lost without this sexy-shaped vessel! A must for any aspiring minxologist, this glass has a cone-shaped bowl atop a stem. Cocktails served in a martini glass should be chilled, and the long stem allows the drinker to hold it without affecting the temperature. Pretty cool, huh?

Hurricane Glass

Hold onto your hats! Also known as a tulip glass, this generally holds punches and frozen drinks. It's similarly shaped to a vase and is typically taller and wider than a highball glass.

Margarita Coupette

Similar to a martini glass but larger and curved.

Pitcher/Jug

A large container, usually with a handle and spout for pouring, that holds many servings.

Wine Glass

A glass that, er, holds wine.

Champagne Coupe

Often stacked in layers to build a champagne tower at weddings, this broad-bowled glass is also known as the Marie Antoinette, so named as it's said to be shaped around the curve of her breast. Let them drink champagne!

Champagne Flute

A tall, narrow glass that houses the bubbly stuff. Cheers!

PINK
PRE-DRINKS

"Pink isn't just a colour it's an attitude"

Miley Cyrus

CLASSIC COSMOPOLITAN

"Hi, I'd like a cheeseburger, please, large fries and a Cosmopolitan" – Carrie Bradshaw

Made popular by the sassy TV show *Sex and the City*, this cocktail is just as delicious with fancy hors d'oeuvres as it is with fast food.

35 ML/1¼ OZ LEMON VODKA
20 ML/⅔ OZ TRIPLE SEC
20 ML/⅔ OZ FRESHLY SQUEEZED LIME JUICE
25 ML/1 OZ CRANBERRY JUICE
LEMON PEEL, TO GARNISH (OPTIONAL)

SERVES 1

Add all the ingredients to a shaker filled with ice, shake sharply and strain into a chilled martini glass. Garnish with lemon peel for that extra zing!

SEA BREEZE

A beach-themed party would be the perfect time to serve this cranberry concoction. And if it's served by a surfer dude with abs that won't quit, so much the better.

25 ML/⅔ OZ VODKA
150 ML/5 OZ CRANBERRY JUICE
50 ML/2 OZ FRESHLY SQUEEZED GRAPEFRUIT JUICE
A LIME WEDGE, TO GARNISH
ICE CUBES, TO SERVE

SERVES 1

Half-fill a tall glass with ice. Pour in the vodka and add the cranberryand grapefruit juices. Stir and garnish with a lime wedge. Serve immediately.

LEGEND

Surrounded by your bachelorettes – each a legend in their own right – what drink could be more apt?

50 ML/2 OZ VODKA
25 ML/1 OZ CREME DE MURE
25 ML/1 OZ FRESHLY SQUEEZED LIME JUICE
1 DASH SUGAR SYRUP
LEMON PEEL, TO GARNISH (OPTIONAL)

SERVES 1

Add all the ingredients to a shaker filled with ice, shake sharply and strain into a chilled martini glass. Garnish with lemon peel.

CLOVER CLUB

The four-leaf clover is deemed good luck.
Why not feed the bride-to-be four of these
raspberry-based cocktails to wish her all the best
for the future?!

50 ML/2 OZ GIN
20 ML/⅔ OZ FRESHLY SQUEEZED LEMON JUICE
10 ML/2 BARSPOONS RASPBERRY SYRUP
1 DASH EGG WHITE
SUGAR SYRUP, TO TASTE

SERVES 1

Add all the ingredients to a shaker filled with ice and shake
sharply. Strain into a chilled cocktail glass.

GIN BRAMBLE

Reminisce about all the 'prickly' situations you and your girls have gotten yourselves into (and hopefully out of) over the years with this refreshing tipple.

50 ML/2 OZ GIN
25 ML/1 OZ FRESHLY SQUEEZED LEMON JUICE
10 ML/2 BARSPOONS SUGAR SYRUP
CRUSHED ICE, TO SERVE
15 ML/½ OZ CREME DE MURE

TO GARNISH
A LEMON WEDGE
A BLACKCURRANT

SERVES 1

Build the gin, lemon juice and sugar syrup over crushed ice in a rocks glass and stir. Drizzle the crème de mure over the ice and garnish with a lemon wedge and a fresh blackcurrant.

THE KNICKERBOCKER

Serve this fruity punch alongside knickerbocker glory ice cream sundaes for the ultimate indulgence and grab a spoon.

2 BARSPOONS RASPBERRY SYRUP

50 ML/2 OZ SANTA CRUZ RUM

25 ML/1 OZ ORANGE CURAÇAO

20 ML/⅔ OZ FRESHLY SQUEEZED LEMON JUICE

15 ML/½ OZ FRESHLY SQUEEZED LIME JUICE

FRESH RASPBERRIES, TO GARNISH

SERVES 1

Add the raspberry syrup to a cocktail shaker with the rum and curaçao and fill with ice. Squeeze in the juice from the lemon and limes, and drop the spent husks in too. Shake the mixture together.

Strain the drink into a stemmed cocktail glass and serve garnished with fresh raspberries.

DIABLO

Get the gals to don some cheeky horns as
they gulp this long tequila-riddled cocktail.
It's devilishly delicious.

50 ML/2 OZ GOLD TEQUILA
15 ML/½ OZ FRESH LIME
15 ML/½ OZ CREME DE CASSIS
GINGER ALE, TO TOP UP
CRUSHED ICE, TO SERVE
REDCURRANTS, TO GARNISH

SERVES 1

Build all the ingredients in a hurricane glass filled with crushed
ice. Garnish with a small bunch of redcurrants and a devil fork
swizzle stick.

RED CACTUS

Chill in 'Margaritaville' with this drink that packs
a zesty punch. And if you happen to sample
it before the guests arrive... so what?
It's 5 o'clock somewhere!

50 ML/2 OZ SAUZA EXTRA GOLD TEQUILA
20 ML/⅔ OZ TRIPLE SEC
20 ML/⅔ OZ CHAMBORD
35 ML/1¼ OZ FRESHLY SQUEEZED LIME JUICE
4 FRESH RASPBERRIES
LIME SLICES, TO GARNISH

SERVES 1

Add all the ingredients to a blender. Add two cups of crushed
ice and blend for 20 seconds. Pour into a margarita coupette
or hurricane glass. Garnish with lime slices and serve.

BERRY CAIPIROSKA

Juicy gossip + juicy cocktail = a salacious night.

50 ML/2 OZ VODKA

4 LIME WEDGES

2 WHITE SUGAR CUBES

3 FRESH BERRIES, PLUS EXTRA TO GARNISH
(STRAWBERRIES, RASPBERRIES OR BLUEBERRIES)

CRUSHED ICE, TO SERVE

SERVES 1

Muddle all the ingredients in a rock glass with a wooden
pestle. Top up with crushed ice and stir gently to mix. Serve
garnished with a few fresh berries skewered onto
a toothpick/cocktail stick.

For extra zing:

The Caipiroska is an elegant twist on the classic Caipirinha,
using vodka instead of the usual cachaça. If preferred, omit
the berries and add extra lime for a more citrussy tipple.

BACARDI COCKTAIL

There's something very liberating –
and a bit naughty – about smoking a cigar.
Use this rum cocktail to inspire a few puffs
on a fine Cuban specimen.

50 ML/2 OZ BACARDI WHITE RUM
3 BARSPOONS GRENADINE
20 ML/⅔ OZ FRESHLY SQUEEZED LIME JUICE

SERVES 1

Shake all the ingredients sharply over ice, then strain into
a chilled martini glass and serve.

DARK & STRAWMY

Tall, dark and... fruity! It's just what you've always
wanted in a man, sorry, cocktail.

3 LIME SLICES
2 STRAWBERRIES, SLICED PLUS EXTRA TO GARNISH
ICE CUBES, TO SERVE
50 ML/2 OZ DARK RUM
GINGER ALE, TO TOP UP

SERVES 1

Muddle the lime and the strawberries in a highball glass.
Add ice and the remaining ingredients and stir gently.
Serve with a straw and half a strawberry to garnish.

COMMODORE COCKTAIL

The frothy cloud sitting atop this tipple is achieved by the egg white and lends a fluffy lightness that helps it slip down effortlessly. This drink is rich, smooth and sweet – just like the naval commodore who serves it (a girl can dream, can't she?).

50 ML/2 OZ LIGHT PUERTO RICAN-STYLE RUM
25 ML/1 OZ FRESHLY SQUEEZED LEMON JUICE
10 ML/2 BARSPOONS GRENADINE
10 ML/2 BARSPOONS RASPBERRY SYRUP
5 ML/1 BARSPOON CASTER/SUPERFINE SUGAR
1 EGG WHITE

SERVES 1

Add all ingredients to a cocktail shaker filled with ice and shake sharply to blend and whip up the egg white. Strain into a frosted coupette glass and serve immediately while the froth is still at it's best.

SHIRLEY TEMPLE

Roll out the pink carpet with this sweet thirst-quencher, named after 'America's Little Darling' – one of Hollywood's most notable childhood stars.

25 ML/1 OZ GRENADINE
ICE CUBES, TO SERVE
GINGER ALE OR LEMON SODA, TO TOP UP
A LEMON WEDGE, TO GARNISH

SERVES 1

Pour the grenadine into a highball glass filled with ice and top with either ginger ale or lemon soda. Garnish with lemon wedge and serve.

PINK
MARTINIS

"It's about being alive and feisty and not sitting down
and shutting up, even if people would like you to"

Pink

METROPOLITAN

This cocktail oozes sophistication, class and good taste. Just like the fashionistas who'll be supping it. Ahem.

35 ML/1¼ OZ ABSOLUT KURANT VODKA OR OTHER BLACKCURRANT FLAVOURED SPIRIT
20 ML/⅔ OZ TRIPLE SEC
20 ML/⅔ OZ FRESHLY SQUEEZED LIME JUICE
25 ML/1 OZ CRANBERRY JUICE
ORANGE PEEL, TO GARNISH

SERVES 1

Shake all the ingredients sharply over ice and strain into a chilled martini glass.

To make a flaming orange peel, squeeze the oil from a strip of orange peel, held skin downwards and over a flame above the glass. Rub the rim with the orange peel before dropping it into the glass.

PONTBERRY MARTINI

This cocktail was created in the late '90s for the opening of sexy lingerie shop Agent Provocateur in Pont Street, London. Ooh, la la!

50 ML/2 OZ VODKA
75 ML/2½ OZ CRANBERRY JUICE
A LARGE DASH OF CREME DE MURE

SERVES 1

Shake all the ingredients in a shaker filled with ice. Strain into a pre-chilled martini glass and serve.

RASPBERRY MARTINI

When gals gather, the subject of exes will inevitably crop up. With every taste of this thick martini, blow a metaphorical raspberry their way. Mature? No. Satisfying? Absolutely.

50 ML/2 OZ VODKA
A DASH OF FRAMBOISE
A DASH OF ORANGE BITTERS
12.5 ML/½ OZ RASPBERRY PUREE
2 FRESH RASPBERRIES, TO GARNISH

SERVES 1

Shake all the ingredients in a shaker filled with ice and strain into a pre-chilled martini glass. Garnish with two raspberries.

WATERMELON MARTINI

Who could forget the immortal line of Baby
in Dirty Dancing: "I carried a watermelon"? Cringe!
Play this classic movie while you're being
pampered and give Baby a consolatory 'Cheers'
when she utters these words.

1 CUP SLICED RIPE WATERMELON, PLUS A SLICE TO GARNISH
50 ML/2 OZ VODKA
1 CUP ICE
SUGAR SYRUP, TO TASTE

SERVES 1

Muddle the watermelon in a mixing glass, add the vodka and ice
and shake sharply. Strain into a chilled martini glass and garnish
with a slice of watermelon. Add sugar syrup if desired.

HIBISCUS MARTINI

The hibiscus flower is big, bold, bright
and beautiful. Not only does it make a blooming
marvelous cocktail, it also makes a gorgeous hair
accessory. Simply tuck one behind your ear
and you're good to go.

25 ML/1 OZ VODKA
5 ML/1 BARSPOON FRESHLY SQUEEZED LIME JUICE
A DASH OF FRAMBOISE LIQUEUR
50 ML/2 OZ HIBISCUS CORDIAL
500 G/2½ CUPS CASTER/GRANULATD SUGAR
A HIBISCUS FLOWER OR PETAL, TO GARNISH

SERVES 1

Add all the ingredients to a shaker filled with ice, shake sharply
and strain into a pre-chilled martini glass. Garnish with
a hibiscus flower.

BLOOD MARTINI

Twilight fan? Discuss the highs, lows and steamy
bits of Bella's and Edward's relationship while
sucking down this bittersweet blend.

50 ML/2 OZ VODKA
15 ML/½ OZ CAMPARI
10 ML/2 BARSPOONS FRAMBOISE
5 ML/1 BARSPOON FRESHLY SQUEEZED LIME JUICE
30 ML/1 OZ PLUS 1 BARSPOON CRANBERRY JUICE
A DASH OF COINTREAU
A FLAMING ORANGE PEEL (SEE PAGE 48), TO GARNISH

SERVES 1

Add all the ingredients to a shaker filled with ice, shake sharply
and strain into a pre-chilled martini glass.

Garnish with a flaming orange peel (see page 48).

CHEESECAKE MARTINI

You'll need a spoon with this one – it's effectively an alcoholic dessert (yum!)

1 DIGESTIVE BISCUIT/GRAHAM CRACKER
10 ML/2 BARSPOONS SUGAR SYRUP
50 ML/2 OZ VODKA
12.5 ML/½ OZ CHAMBORD
12.5 ML/½ OZ RASPBERRY PUREE
12.5 ML/½ OZ DOUBLE/HEAVY CREAM

SERVES 1

Grind the biscuit/cracker into crumbs, add the sugar syrup, mix and pack into the bottom of a martini glass. Put the remaining ingredients into a shaker, shake and strain gently over the crumbs into the martini glass.

FEISTY FEMININE
FIZZ

"I don't think I will ever get tired of wearing pink"

Emma Bunton

ROSSINI

Bring a little Italian culture to your get-together
with this classy bevvy. Named after the Italian
opera composer Gioacchino Antonio Rossini,
you could always play his music in the background
(after you've got your Beyoncé fix, obvs).

15 ML/½ OZ RASPBERRY PUREE
5 ML/1 BARSPOON CHAMBORD (OPTIONAL)
2 DASHES OF ORANGE BITTERS
CHAMPAGNE, TO TOP UP

SERVES 1

Add the purée, Chambord (if using) and bitters to a champagne
flute and top up with champagne. Stir gently and serve.

COSMO ROYALE

A bundle of joy on its way calls for some champers, which just so happens to be the key ingredient to give this exceptional cocktail a fizzy spin.

35 ML/1¼ OZ LEMON VODKA
15 ML/½ OZ FRESHLY SQUEEZED LIME JUICE
15 ML/½ OZ COINTREAU
25 ML/1 OZ CRANBERRY JUICE
CHAMPAGNE, TO FLOAT
ORANGE PEEL, TO GARNISH

SERVES 1

Add all the ingredients, except the champagne, to a shaker filled with ice. Shake sharply and strain into a chilled martini glass. Float the champagne on the surface and garnish with orange peel.

ABSOLUTELY FABULOUS MARTINI

"Patsy darling, do you want a cocktail"
– Eddie Monsoon

Of course she does! Made famous by the iconic
TV show, this 'Bolli Stoli' cocktail is ab fab, sweetie.

25 ML/1 OZ STOLICHNYA VODKA
10 ML/2 BARSPOONS FRAISE DE BOIS
35 ML/1¼ OZ CRANBERRY JUICE
CHAMPAGNE, TO TOP UP
½ STRAWBERRY, TO GARNISH

SERVES 1

Add all the ingredients, except the champagne,
to a shaker filled with ice.

Shake sharply and strain into a pre-chilled martini glass.
Top with champagne. Garnish with a strawberry and serve.

RASPBERRY RICKEY

Raspberries are said to contain about 50%
of the recommended daily allowance of Vitamin C.
So, the more of these cocktails you drink, the
healthier you're being, right?

4 FRESH RASPBERRIES
ICE CUBES, TO SERVE
50 ML/2 OZ VODKA
20 ML/⅔ OZ FRESHLY SQUEEZED LIME JUICE
1 DASH CHAMBORD
SODA WATER, TO TOP UP
A LIME WEDGE, TO GARNISH

SERVES 1

Muddle the raspberries in the bottom of a highball glass.
Fill with ice, add the remaining ingredients and stir gently.
Garnish with a lime wedge and serve with two straws.

SLOE GIN FIZZ

Live life in the sloe lane with this tasty 'tail that makes no apologies for its distinctive taste.

50 ML/2 OZ SLOE GIN
20 ML/⅔ OZ FRESHLY SQUEEZED LEMON JUICE
A DASH SUGAR SYRUP
SODA WATER, TO TOP UP
ICE CUBES, TO SERVE
A LEMON SLICE, TO GARNISH

SERVES 1

Add all the ingredients, except the soda, to a shaker filled with ice. Shake sharply and strain into a highball glass filled with ice. Top with soda water, garnish with a lemon slice and serve with two straws.

KIR ROYAL

Want to suggest names for the buba? This simple drink could inspire a few: Kirsten, Kirsty, Kira, Kirby, Kirstin, Kiri...

1 DASH CREME DE CASSIS
CHAMPAGNE, TO TOP UP

SERVES 1

Add a small dash of crème de cassis to a champagne flute and gently top with champagne. Stir gently and serve.

STRAWBERRY MULE

Break the ice with this fruitier version of the classic Moscow Mule. To up the cute factor, serve it in Eeyore glasses.

2 THIN SLICES OF FRESH GINGER

3 STRAWBERRIES, PLUS 1 EXTRA TO GARNISH

50 ML/2 OZ VODKA

15 ML/½ OZ CREME DE FRAISE

A DASH OF SUGAR SYRUP

GINGER BEER, TO TOP UP

TO SERVE

ICE CUBES

LIME PEEL

SERVES 1

Put the ginger and strawberries together in a cocktail shaker and pound with a wooden muddler. Add the vodka, crème de fraise and sugar syrup and replace the lid. Shake briskly, then strain into a tall glass filled with ice. Top up with ginger beer, stir gently and garnish with a strawberry and lime peel to serve.

HAMPTONS HANGOVER

Weekending in the Hamptons? Probably not, right? Why not play make-believe and imagine you're members of the glitterati with this fragrant summer cocktail?

30 ML/1 OZ PLUS 1 BARSPOON CREME DE CASSIS
60 ML/2⅓ OZ ROSE SYRUP, SUCH AS MONIN
20 ML/⅔ OZ FRESHLY SQUEEZED LEMON JUICE
CLEAR SPARKLING LEMONADE, TO TOP UP
ICE CUBES, TO SERVE

SERVES 1

Half-fill a tumbler with ice. Add the cassis, rose syrup and lemon juice. Top up with lemonade and stir gently before serving.

GRAPEFRUIT ROSE SPARKLE

A sweet treat for the mother-to-be. Nine months without a snifter can take its toll... this non-alcoholic fizz will put a smile on her face, fo shiz.

480 ML/4 OZ RUBY RED GRAPEFRUIT JUICE, CHILLED
20 ML/⅔ OZ ROSE-FLOWER WATER, CHILLED
5 ML/1 BARSPOON AGAVE NECTAR
½ RUBY RED GRAPEFRUIT, PEELED AND SEGMENTED
120 ML/4¼ OZ SODA WATER

SERVES 4

Combine the grapefruit juice, rose-flower water, agave nectar and red grapefruit in a large jug/pitcher.

Divide the grapefruit pulp between 4 champagne flutes (or similar) and finish with a splash of soda water.
Serve immediately.

RASPBERRY & APPLE FIZZ

Ms. Preggers isn't just expecting a baby... she's also expecting a yummy drink at her baby shower. This magic mocktail will deliver (and hopefully she won't until after the party!).

300 G/2 CUPS FROZEN RASPBERRIES
250 ML/8 OZ APPLE JUICE
SPARKLING WATER, TO TOP UP

TO SERVE
ICE CUBES
APPLE SLICES

SERVES 4

Put the raspberries, apple juice and ice cubes in a blender or liquidizer and whizz until smooth.

Pour into 4 tall glasses and top up with sparkling water. Garnish with thin slices of apple and a serve with a straw.

PERKY PUNCHES
& PITCHERS

"Anything is possible with sunshine and a little pink"

Lilly Pulitzer

CLASSIC SANGRIA

This red-wine punch is fabulously fruity and will transport you to balmy climes with one sip.

2 ORANGES, SLICED

2 LEMONS, SLICED

½ TABLESPOON CASTER/GRANULATED SUGAR, TO TASTE

2 X 750-ML/25-OZ BOTTLES RED WINE

165 ML/5½ OZ GRAND MARNIER

1 APPLE, SLICED INTO THIN WEDGES

ICE CUBES, TO SERVE

CLEAR SPARKLING LEMONADE, TO TOP UP

SERVES 6

Place half the orange and lemon slices in a large jug/pitcher and sprinkle over the sugar. Leave to macerate for 15 minutes then add the wine and Grand Marnier and chill in the fridge for 1 hour.

When ready to serve, add the apple wedges and remaining orange and lemon slices. Add a few cups of ice and top up with lemonade to taste. Stir and pour into tall glasses to serve, spooning a little fruit into each, if desired.

PEACH & STRAWBERRY SANGRIA

A more fragrant, subtle version of the classic sangria, this drink is a real peach!

2 FRESH PEACHES, STONED AND THINLY SLICED
250 G/2 CUPS STRAWBERRIES, HULLED AND SLICED
1 ORANGE, SLICED
150 ML/5 OZ CREME DE FRAISE
2 X 750-ML/25-OZ BOTTLES DRY WHITE WINE
1 SMALL CUCUMBER, PEELED, DESEEDED AND THINLY SLICED
CLEAR SPARKLING LEMONADE, TO TOP UP
BORAGE FLOWERS, TO GARNISH (OPTIONAL)
ICE CUBES, TO SERVE

SERVES 6

Put the peaches, strawberries and orange slices in a large jug/pitcher with the strawberry liqueur. Pour in the wine and chill for 30 minutes. When ready to serve, add the cucumber and some ice and top up with lemonade. Pour into glasses and garnish each serving with borage flowers, if desired.

TRIPLE GODDESS

You'll be once, twice, three times a lady. with this yummy mocktail that exudes a tangy effervescence.

300 ML/10 OZ POMEGRANATE JUICE
300 ML/10 OZ CLOUDY APPLE JUICE
FRESHLY SQUEEZED JUICE OF 6 LIMES
50 ML/2 OZ ELDERFLOWER CORDIAL
SPARKLING MINERAL WATER, TO TOP UP
APPLE FANS, TO GARNISH
ICE CUBES, TO SERVE

SERVES 4

Add the fruit juices and elderflower cordial to a large jug/pitcher and stir gently to mix. Top up with mineral water and serve over ice garnished with an apple fan.

TOM COLLINS

Tom Hardy... Tom Brady... Tom Cruise (in his day)... There's no denying that Toms are cool! Add Tom Collins, this zesty, refreshing cocktail to the list and serve over ice to chill your guests out.

500 ML/17 OZ GIN

FRESHLY SQUEEZED JUICE OF 6 LEMONS

125 ML/4⅓ OZ FRESH FRUIT PUREE
(POMEGRANATE, RASPBERRY OR BLUEBERRY)

125 ML/4⅓ OZ SUGAR SYRUP

ICE CUBES, TO SERVE

SODA WATER, TO TOP UP

SEASONAL FRESH FRUIT, TO GARNISH

SERVES 10

Add all the ingredients except the soda water to a pitcher or punch bowl filled with ice and stir gently to mix. Top up with soda water and stir again. Serve in tall ice-filled glasses, garnished with fresh fruit.

WATERMELON & CINNAMON PUNCH

There's a reason slices of watermelon look like huge smiles: they can't fail to make you happy, especially on a hot summer's day. Add cinnamon to the mix and you're in for an all-out joy fest.

2 LARGE WATERMELONS, PEELED AND ROUGHLY CHOPPED
FRESHLY SQUEEZED JUICE OF 8 LIMES
200 ML/7 OZ CINNAMON-INFUSED SYRUP
1 CUP CRUSHED ICE
SPARKLING MINERAL WATER, TO TOP UP

SERVES 10

Put the watermelon in a blender with the lime juice, cinnamon syrup and crushed ice. Blend until smooth.

Pour the watermelon mixture into a punch bowl and add a block of ice. Top up with sparkling mineral water, stir, and serve.

POMEGRANATE PUNCH

Babicka is a unique Czech vodka infused with wormwood (the key ingredient of absinthe) so too many glasses of this pink drink and you'll wind up punch-drunk!

500 ML/17 OZ BABICKA VODKA
750 ML/25 OZ POMEGRANATE JUICE
FRESHLY SQUEEZED JUICE OF 5 GRAPEFRUITS
FRESHLY SQUEEZED JUICE OF 8 LIMES
150 ML/5 OZ SUGAR SYRUP
500 ML/17 OZ SODA WATER, TO SERVE
PARED GRAPEFRUIT ZEST AND FRESH MINT SPRIGS, TO GARNISH

SERVES 10

Put the vodka, the pomegranate, grapefruit, and lime juices, and the sugar syrup in a large punch bowl or pitcher filled with ice. Top up with soda water, and stir gently to mix. Serve in ice-filled highball glasses, garnished with a grapefruit zest spiral and sprigs of mint.

CRANBERRY & FRUIT PUNCH

Designated drivers, teetotalers, preggers women and kids alike can guzzle this punch to their hearts' content as there's no alcohol included. 0% booze, 100% delish.

250 G/2 CUPS MIXED FRESH BERRIES, PLUS EXTRA TO SERVE
(STRAWBERRIES, RASPBERRIES OR BLUEBERRIES)
1 ORANGE, SLICED
2 LITRES/68 OZ CRANBERRY JUICE
1 SMALL CUCUMBER, PEELED, DESEEDED AND SLICED
SPARKLING WATER OR CLEAR SPARKLING LEMONADE, TO TOP UP

SERVES 12

Put the berries, orange slices and cranberry juice in a large jug/pitcher and chill in the fridge for 1 hour. When ready to serve, add the cucumber and some ice and top up with sparkling water. Pour into tall glasses or tumblers and garnish with a few fresh berries skewered onto a toothpick/cocktail stick.

BAY BREEZE

This uncomplicated cocktail is breezy, tease-y and easy peasy lemon squeezy (well, technically cranberry and pineapple squeezy!).

200 ML/7 OZ GOLDEN RUM
400 ML/14 OZ CRANBERRY JUICE
200 ML/7 OZ PINEAPPLE JUICE
ICE CUBES, TO SERVE
LIME WEDGES, TO GARNISH

SERVES 4

Add all the ingredients to a large jug/pitcher filled with ice, stir and serve in highball glasses filled with ice garnished with a lime wedge.

SILK STOCKING

Add a little 'ooh la la' to your afternoon tea with
this mischievous mélange of velvety indulgence.

150 ML/5 OZ GOLD TEQUILA
60 ML/3 OZ WHITE CREME DE CACAO
20 ML/⅔ OZ GRENADINE
60 ML/3 OZ DOUBLE/HEAVY CREAM
2 FRESH RASPBERRIES, TO GARNISH

SERVES 4

Add all the ingredients to a blender. Add two cups of crushed
ice and blend for 20 seconds. Pour the mixture into a martini
glass, garnish with two raspberries and serve.

COSMOPOLITAN ICED TEA

Is it a classy cocktail?

Is it a refreshing sweetened tea?

Is it a scrumdiddlyumptious drink simply perfect for a summer tea party? Yes, yes and yes.

120 ML/4 OZ VODKA, VANILLA-FLAVOURED IF AVAILABLE
60 ML/2¼ OZ TRIPLE SEC
320 ML/10⅔ OZ CRANBERRY JUICE
FRESHLY SQUEEZED JUICE OF 2 LIMES
4 SLICES LIME, TO GARNISH

SERVES 4

Add the vodka, triple sec, cranberry and lime juices to a large jug/pitcher filled with ice. Stir well and serve in teacups garnished with a slice of lime.

CRANBERRY, LEMON & GINGER ICED TEA

"Would you like a little more tea?" – Mad Hatter.
Take inspiration from Alice in Wonderland and label
this zingy beverage with a cute 'Drink Me' tag.

4 LEMON AND GINGER-FLAVOURED TEA BAGS

1 LITRE/68 OZ JUST-BOILED WATER

2 TEASPOONS BROWN SUGAR

400 ML/14 OZ CRANBERRY JUICE

1 LEMON, SLICED

ICE CUBES, TO SERVE

SERVES 6

Put the tea bags in a heatproof jug and pour in the just-boiled
water. Leave to steep for about 10 minutes, then remove and
discard the tea bags. Stir in the sugar and let cool. Chill for
1 hour.

Stir in the cranberry juice and add the lemon slices Divide
between tall, ice-filled glasses to serve.

STRAWBERRY, ROSE & VANILLA ICED TEA

Deliciously delicate and downright dainty, this mouth-watering fusion of all things scrummy can be topped off with romantic rose petals.

2 TABLESPOONS STRAWBERRY-FLAVOURED TEA INFUSION
1 VANILLA POD/BEAN, SPLIT LENGTHWAYS
1 LITRE/68 OZ JUST-BOILED WATER
2 TABLESPOONS ROSEWATER
250 G/2 CUPS STRAWBERRIES, HULLED AND SLICED
CLEAR SPARKLING LEMONADE, TO TOP UP
ROSE PETALS, TO GARNISH (OPTIONAL)
ICE CUBES, TO SERVE

SERVES 6

Place the strawberry tea and vanilla pod in a heatproof jug/bowl and add the water. Stir well and leave to steep until cold. Strain the tea into a clean jug/pitcher and stir in the rosewater. Add some strawberries to 6 ice-filled glasses and pour over the tea. Top up with lemonade and garnish with a few rose petals to serve.

BERRY CORDIAL

'Cordially invite' your guests to enjoy this blended-berry beverage that fizzes and refreshes... it'll be like a party in their mouths.

500 G/4 CUPS FRESH MIXED BERRIES
(RASPBERRIES, STRAWBERRIES, BLUEBERRIES OR BLACKCURRANTS)
125 ML/4 OZ SUGAR SYRUP
FRESHLY SQUEEZED JUICE OF ½ LIME
SPARKLING WATER, TO TOP UP
A FEW WHOLE BERRIES, TO GARNISH
ICE CUBES, TO SERVE

SERVES 4

Place the berries, sugar syrup and lime juice in a blender or liquidizer and whizz until smooth. Pass the mixture through a fine sieve/strainer and divide the cordial between 4 tall glasses.

Add ice cubes, top up with sparkling water and garnish with a few berries to serve.

SASSY SHAKES
& SMOOTHIES

"I believe in pink"

Audrey Hepburn

RASPBERRY, APPLE & LYCHEE JUICE

Rehydrate with this juicily delectable drink containing antioxidants galore, along with properties to help alleviate a cough thanks to the lychee juice. Healthy just got a whole lot tastier.

200 G/1½ CUPS FROZEN RASPBERRIES
565 G/4⅓ CUPS CANNED LYCHEES, DRAINED
250 ML/8½ OZ APPLE JUICE

SERVES 2

Put all the ingredients in a blender and blend until smooth.

BERRY SMOOTHIE

Replenish your energy levels with this jumble of juices. The berries provide sumptuous sweetness... but if you need a little more, simply add more honey, honey.

8-10 FRESH BERRIES OF YOUR CHOICE
(STRAWBERRIES, BLACKBERRIES OR RASPBERRIES)

2 TABLESPOONS BERRY OR STRAWBERRY SAUCE

300 ML/10 OZ NATURAL YOGURT

300 ML/10 OZ MILK, CHILLED

150 G/1 CUP FRESH RIPE STRAWBERRIES

250 G/2 CUPS FROZEN SUMMER BERRIES

1 TEASPOON PURE VANILLA EXTRACT

1 TABLESPOON RUNNY HONEY, OR TO TASTE

SERVES 2

Put the berry sauce in a squeezy bottle and pipe a spiral onto the inside of each glass. Put the yogurt and milk in a blender, add the strawberries, frozen berries, vanilla extract and honey and blitz until all the fruit is blended. Pass the smoothie through a sieve/strainer to remove the seeds, then pour into the prepared glasses. Thread several berries onto a skewer and add to each glass with a straw and serve.

MANGO BERRY PASH

What are you passionate about? One taste of this two-tone tropical treat alongside your granola and your answer will most likely be, "This drink!"

100 G/⅔ CUP FROZEN MIXED BERRIES, THAWED

1 TABLESPOON ICING/CONFECTIONERS' SUGAR

1 LARGE MANGO, PEELED AND STONED/PITTED, PLUS EXTRA SLICES TO SERVE

THE FLESH OF 1 PASSION FRUIT, HALVED

SPARKLING WATER, TO TOP UP

ICE CUBES, TO SERVE

SERVES 2

Put the berries in a bowl and stir in the icing/confectioners' sugar, mashing well with a fork. Set aside for 15 minutes, then pass through a fine sieve/strainer. Purée the mango flesh in a blender or liquidizer until smooth and stir in the passion fruit pulp. Put a few ice cubes into 2 tall glasses, add the berry mixture and mango and passion fruit purée and top up with sparkling water and garnish with a slice of mango to serve.

ROSE PETAL DREAM MILKSHAKE

Prepare yourself for a much-deserved afternoon nap with this slumber-inducing shake which, thanks to the calming effects of the lavender, offers up the zzz factor and invites in the land of nod. Sweet dreams.

400 ML/14 OZ MILK, CHILLED

4 SCOOPS ROSE ICE CREAM (SUCH AS KULFI) OR VANILLA ICE CREAM

½ TABLESPOON ROSE SYRUP

FRESH ROSE PETALS, THINLY SHREDDED, TO DECORATE

ROSE TURKISH DELIGHT, TO SERVE

For the Rose Petal Dream, put the milk and ice cream in a blender and blitz until frothy. Add the rose syrup to taste and blitz again. If you are using vanilla ice cream, add an extra spoonful of rose syrup for more rose flavour. Pour into chilled glasses and top with the shredded rose petals. Serve immediately with Turkish delight, if using.

CHOCOLATE & CHERRY FREEZE

Welcome the candyman into your life with this '50s-diner-inspired milkshake and, who knows, your cherry might just pop too.

2 TABLESPOONS CHOCOLATE SYRUP
250 ML/8½ OZ CHERRY JUICE
2 SCOOPS CHERRY FROZEN YOGURT
CANNED WHIPPED CREAM, TO SERVE

TO DECORATE
CHOCOLATE SPRINKLES
2 WHOLE CHERRIES

SERVES 2

Spoon a tablespoon of chocolate syrup into each glass and swirl so that the bottom third of the glass is coated with syrup.

Put the cherry juice and frozen yogurt in a blender and blitz until frothy. Pour into the prepared glasses and top each with a squirt of whipped cream. Decorate the glasses with chocolate sprinkles and a whole cherry and serve immediately.

RASPBERRY RIPPLE

Remember the good ol' days of climbing trees,
making dens and raspberry ripple ice cream
for dessert? Relive your innocent childhood
memories with this sweet soda that's sure
to float your nostalgic boat.

4 SCOOPS RASPBERRY RIPPLE ICE CREAM
10 FRESH RASPBERRIES
500 ML/17 OZ RASPBERRY OR CHERRY SODA, CHILLED
PINK SPRINKLES, TO DECORATE

SERVES 2

Put one scoop of ice cream in the bottom of each glass
and divide the raspberries between them. Top up the
glasses with raspberry or cherry soda and finish with a second
scoop of ice cream. Decorate with sprinkles and serve
immediately with straws.

WATERMELON COOLER

Always fancied yourself as a baller but feel you lack a certain hip-hop cred? Well, this recipe will transform you into the coolest (melon) baller in town. Word.

1 SMALL RIPE SEEDLESS WATERMELON
FRESHLY SQUEEZED JUICE OF 3 LIMES
6 CUPS ICE CUBES
SUGAR, TO TASTE

SERVES 2

Using the melon baller, make 6 balls of melon and thread 3 onto a skewer. Cover the skewers and store in the fridge until needed.

Chop the remaining watermelon flesh and squeeze the juice from the remaining limes (removing any pips). Put the lime juice and watermelon flesh in a blender with the ice cubes and blitz to a smooth purée. Taste the drink for sweetness. If it is too sour, add a little sugar and blend again.

Pour into chilled glasses and serve with straws and melon swizzle sticks.

INDEX